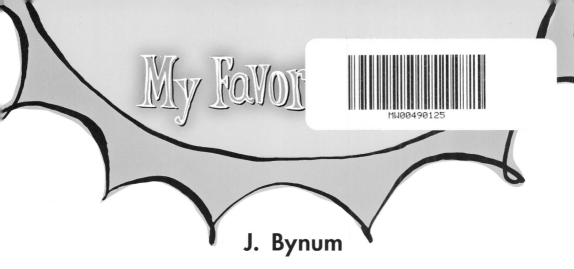

My Favor

J. Bynum

Contents

What is the sun? 4

How big is the sun? 6

Why is daytime light
and nighttime dark? 8

How does the sun help us? 10

Is the sun ever bad for us? 12

Rigby®

A Harcourt Achieve Imprint

www.Rigby.com
1-800-531-5015

Sunrise, sunshine, sunny days...

My name is Cosmo,
and I love the sun.

People always ask me
questions about the sun.

Join me as I shine some light
on why the sun is so special.

What is the sun?

The sun is a star!
It is closer to us
than any other star.
That is why it is so bright.

How big is the sun?

The sun is really, really big.

Driving in a fast car, it would take over three years to drive around the sun.

8

The sun rises in the morning to light up the sky.

At night, the sun goes down. The sky becomes dark.

The sun gives us light.
It is our main source of heat.

Sunshine also helps
our food to grow.

Is the sun ever bad for us?

Yes, the sun is very hot.
Remember to wear sun block!

All of these questions
have made me
remember one more
important fact...

Just how much I love to have fun in the sun!

The Solar System

Neptune

Uranus

Saturn

Jupiter

Mars

Earth

Venus

Mercury

SUN